Stars of Serendipity

by
Amelia E.
Eric-Markovic

Stars of Serendipity
Copyright © 2023 by Amelia E. Eric-Markovic.
All rights reserved. No part of this publication may be reproduced, stored or transmitted in any form or by any means, electronic, mechanical, photocopying, recording, scanning, or otherwise without written permission from the publisher. It is illegal to copy this book, post it to a website, or distribute it by any other means without permission.

First Edition 2023
ISBN: 978-1-7390487-0-9

Cover Design: Niokoba
Artwork: Niokoba
Beta Reader: Allison Sigmon

Thank you to the killers, the kind, and the contemplators, and for every moment when you find good things without searching for them.

Stars of Serendipity

CONTENTS

The Killer

New Times, New Ashes 10
Shy Teeth 11
Greedy Robbed 12
Underground Instinct... 14
Sound Soldier 15
Gratitude in Transformation...................................... 16
Boasting 101 17
Mustache Machete.. 18
Manhood 19
Pretty Hurricane 20
Priceless Pride 22
Money Problems... 23
Feminine Fear... 24
Switching Realms 25
Gladiator Goddess 27
Infernal Encounters... 28
New Times, New Ashes 29
Honest Rage.. 30
Personal Setback...31
Masquerading Monstrosity 32
A Kaleidoscope of Warnings 33
Palm Raider 34
Sweet Labyrinth 35
Mourning Kiss 36

Top Shelf Flats 37
Vile Moon 38
Unbalanced Equation 40
Ctrl + C 41
Societies Definitions 42
Unconsciously Thrown In 43
Vintage Tragedy 44
Buried Betrayal 45
Weighing Emotions 46
Resilient Relapse 48
New Times, New Ashes 49
Grave Farewell 50

The Kind

Cherry Tree 52
Embrace 53
Keepsake 54
"Self-Care" 55
Nurturing Serenity 56
Trial By Tower 57
Compassion Costume 58
Seeing XX 60
Returning Time 61
Giving Thieves 62
Working Life Out 64

Whispers of Perception 65
Mirror Representation 66
Bottled Aspirations... 67
Working Memory 69
Subliminal Help.. 70
Connection Loading 71
Seasons Feelings Change 72
Waking Possession 73
Memories Waltz... 74
That Is All 76
Power of Love 77
Roots of Manhood 79
Presently Past It... 80
Origami Conversations.. 81
Thornless Blooms 82
Devoted Luminary... 84
Timely Acknowledgements 85
Sidus Salutations 86
Angel's Exit 88

The Contemplator

Pointing Back... 90
Parallel Potentials.. 91
Proud Party 92
Feel, Feeling, Felt 93
Hard Pill.. 94
Grieving Nothing 95
Siding With Shapes.. 96

Personal Purge	97
Gifts of Existence	99
Idle Avenue	100
Calling 463	101
Standing Up	102
Musical Feelings	103
Lessons of Reciprocity	104
Glorious Solitude	105
Open A Book	106
Phone Book	108
Growing Pains	109
Stand Alone	111
Caving Chipped	112
Synonyms for Student	113
Intrinsic Treasures	114
A Step Above	115
Gaslighting Orange	116
Paper Echoes	117
Passing Anxieties	118
Glass Crown	120
Plaster Contracts	121
Removing Myself	122
Going Forward	123
Serendipity	124
About the Author	126

The Killer

These individuals serve as catalysts, shaking the very core of our lives and compelling us to confront the depths of our being. They embody the authentic, transformative, and unsettling spirit of human connections. Reflecting on these profound interactions often leaves us unnerved, yet it is precisely this discomfort that propels us forward in our personal growth and self-discovery. These exceptional individuals act as "killers" of complacency, pushing us towards personal change and self-improvement.

NEW TIMES, NEW ASHES

Looking at the hour
feels even
when I am counting down the beats
till you flatline
and I can finally listen to my heart.
pt.I

*Amelia E.
Eric-Markovic*

SHY TEETH

It's hard to know how sincere your smile is
when you don't show your teeth.
Granted you hadn't sharpened your fangs enough
to display them
or whitened them enough
to hide the blood stains.
It's hard to smile with teeth,
when you only use them to kill.

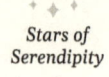

Stars of Serendipity

GREEDY ROBBED

The last seconds on Earth
are counting down slowly.
5
The nose fills with scents
of fresh air and saltwater,
roses and baby's breath,
pine and maple,
and fresh laundry.
4
You can taste
your favourite breakfast on your tongue,
pancakes, strawberries, bacon, eggs,
sweet and filling.
3
Music fills the ears,
blissful and echoing,
ringing through the chambers of the canal.
2
You latch onto their embrace,
warm and comforting.

*Amelia E.
Eric-Markovic*

1
Sparkling lights and vivid colours cover the cornea.

Grasping for the best moments,
the senses are overwhelmed
and the world goes dark.

Is it a felony if Death robs the greedy?

Stars of Serendipity

UNDERGROUND INSTINCT

Crawling up
from the pit in my stomach
navigating the curling of my insides
prowled my intuitions after seeing you.
I slip it under my tongue as we make conversation
so it crawls into the back of my throat
strangling my thoughts and words,
your ego is fed by my breathlessness.
As it makes its way up to my brain
it hides society's rules that
this person should be trustworthy
and projects the truth
on the back of my eyes
so I could finally see
what to do with you.
Save me.

*Amelia E.
Eric-Markovic*

SOUND SOLDIER

The day I found my voice
was when I stopped searching
and started growing anew.
My tongue was sliced
as articulation cut through my throat
and found bullseye in your ears.
Comebacks were my backup
as an attitude forged into my armour
and I suddenly began to wear my tone.
Eyes frosting cold and blood boiling,
my demeanour turned me to stone.

Stars of Serendipity

GRATITUDE IN TRANSFORMATION

I hope that she sends me a thank you card
for making you better
for her.

Amelia E.
Eric-Markovic

BOASTING 101

I bet Einstein bragged, even
Newton and Da Vinci.
Maybe that was their greatest achievement.
Helping us realize that bragging was a word
invented by jealous people
to make you feel lesser
by sharing your accomplishments.

Stars of Serendipity

MUSTACHE MACHETE

Every time you lean in for a kiss
I prepare myself for bloodshed.
Bandaids, ointments, and prayers
are equipped and ready.
73 stab wounds,
the upper lip cries for relief
with my skin red and aching.
We do not heal with knives,
please shave next time.

*Amelia E.
Eric-Markovic*

MANHOOD

Please, stop prescribing manhood
for sentimental men.
Telling boys to lift weights
instead of unloading baggage.
Convincing men they would rather
choke while crying
then choke up while crying.
Tying ties so tight they strangle
any sound of emotion.

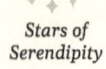

PRETTY HURRICANE

When we met
you welcomed me into your life
hands out,
giving me earbuds to block out the rowdy world.
Your sentences are short and sweet.
Witty commentary and gossip-filled hours.
It was long enough.
Long enough for the wind to rise.
Sirens blare but unable to hear them.
It lasted as long as your sentences
and then it was gone.
You were gone.

Stars of Serendipity

PRICELESS PRIDE

Never try to entice me
with things that I can buy.
My money
on me
looks much better
than your pathetic bribery.

*Amelia E.
Eric-Markovic*

MONEY PROBLEMS

Changing your man
only changes your spendings
and not your problems.

FEMININE FEAR

I know myself,
my titles and designations,
accolades and certifications.
Believe me when I say
that I know what I have done
to impress and astonish the next generation.
But when I ask a man for recognition,
the world crumbles.
Perhaps because I achieved it all
before reaching 21.
Or maybe because I attempted
to do it all on my own,
or they believed they deserved it instead.
But most times, they claim it's
because I am a woman
and every time
I work harder.

*Amelia E.
Eric-Markovic*

SWITCHING REALMS

You love like a sinner,
hiding your affections like a crime
and the sentence was our intertwining.

                               Carrying me with wings spread,
                       you fly towards heaven and drop me halfway,
                          I never anticipated being killed by a saint.

*Amelia E.
Eric-Markovic*

GLADIATOR GODDESS

Grown from oceans and earth,
the girl has no hesitations with standing.
Beauty in gaze,
turns you to stone at a wrong move.
She is powerful and poised.
Sticks and stones bounce off her bones
as words drive her forward,
and the whole room listens.
Egos and masculinity fall at her feet
and she walks over them as if a bridge
to help position herself in misogyny's headquarters.
Women do not bow to boys,
so she stands with men.
Relapsing at how every male that put her down
was never man enough to see her divinity grow.

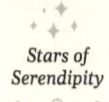

Stars of Serendipity

INFERNAL ENCOUNTERS

The devil lives amongst us.
He hides in rotten fruit and dead plants.
I've seen him lingering around in traffic
and slow walkers.
Once he materialized within shattered toys,
and another time, amidst a forest's fire.
The last time I bumped into him
was in a car accident.
The devil lives among us
in every moment when we see
hell creeping onto earth.

*Amelia E.
Eric-Markovic*

NEW TIMES, NEW ASHES

Looking at the minutes
feels bad
when I am counting down the consequences
till your casket closes
and I can finally open up
pt.II

Stars of Serendipity

HONEST RAGE

I have never been as mad
as the day I was honest with you.
Blind rage is only terrifying if you are a big target,
but aimed shots puncture deeper.
Concise words cut you deep
and examples were your execution.
By the time I was done
I traded the weight of my words
for your bloodshed.

Amelia E. Eric-Markovic

PERSONAL SETBACK

Nothing will set you back
more in life
than the wrong people.
The wrong time will eventually become
the right time.
The wrong place can undervalue you
but the next place may double your worth.
The wrong people will break you
at the wrong time,
in the wrong place,
and leave you.

Stars of Serendipity

MASQUERADING MONSTROSITY

You called yourself Frankenstein,
portraying yourself as a monster
devoid of understanding.
Your stitches became mine
as you pulled apart your seams,
searching your insides for identity.
I struggled to cope with this new creature
as you grapple with my intact form.
Electrocuting your new life into me
until reflections presented strangers;
I saw my spark fading.
With time I found out that
Frankenstein created the monster,
and your title became mine.

*Amelia E.
Eric-Markovic*

A KALEIDOSCOPE OF WARNINGS

Warning flags come in all different colours.
Dyed in our least favourite hues
and if true,
yours would be yellow.
Which makes it harder for me
to believe I ever ignored them.
A colour screaming to slow down,
and yet we sped forward,
as if passing your flags counted as laps in our race
to a perfect relationship.

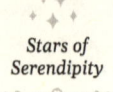
Stars of Serendipity

PALM RAIDER

You grab for my hand
before I can untangle my fingers.
And even when I have nothing left to give
you still stare at my empty palms.

*Amelia E.
Eric-Markovic*

SWEET LABYRINTH

Strawberry shame
and chocolate sins
grace my lips
as I think about how to navigate
the craving for sweetness
seeking balance
for my rotten core.

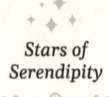

Stars of Serendipity

MOURNING KISS

The light hits my eyes hard
as I blink awake,
pulling you closer
never wanting to leave
the heaven weaved between a fitted sheet
and our covers.
Your eyes unravelled slowly
and your grin fades as the alarm sounds.
The new day has killed our slumbering love again.

*Amelia E.
Eric-Markovic*

TOP SHELF FLATS

Your relationship was like those flats
from when we were younger.
It was pretty at first and great for dates
but when you tried to make them your everyday,
your long-distance,
they hurt you.
And that's why they are better on the top shelf
then as your foundation.

*Stars of
Serendipity*

VILE MOON

I became a phase to you.
Your constant cycling and unwillingness
to show me your everything
eventually, let me return to my light,
with trust issues for those who come and go.

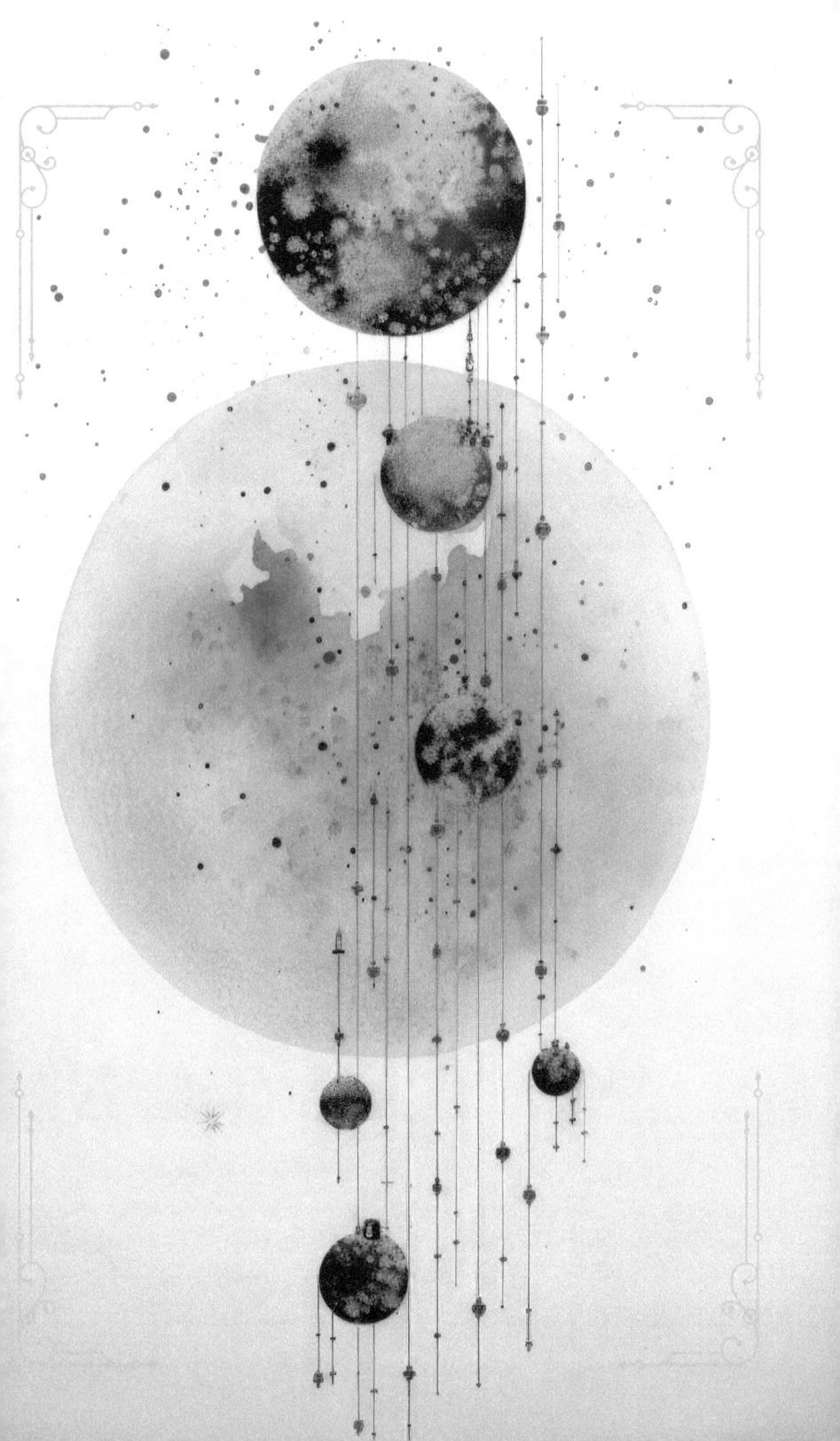

Stars of Serendipity

UNBALANCED EQUATION

Problem-solving
does not work
if one person is the problem
and the other person is the solver.

*Amelia E.
Eric-Markovic*

CTRL + C

Copy and paste
does not work the same
with people.
It is not because we lack control,
but because we cannot save people
in a perfect state.

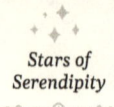
Stars of Serendipity

SOCIETIES DEFINITIONS

Errors:
Permissible to commit,
as long as they can be concealed,
or compensated for.
Look to your last name if you need any assistance.

*Amelia E.
Eric-Markovic*

UNCONSCIOUSLY THROWN IN

"I go beneath the water line
mouth closed, eyes open, ears filled,
and touch empty.
I am void of all sense
yet encumbered with questions.
Floating into the sea of my mind
I swim through my thoughts,
searching for a captain
that went down with my ship;
for the person who misdirected me to crash.
No one stayed for me.
So I sank with my ship."
~ *The unconscious mind grasping for reasons and respiration*

Stars of Serendipity

VINTAGE TRAGEDY

Validating your pain is easier
when they have been convicted
of the same crime before.

*Amelia E.
Eric-Markovic*

BURIED BETRAYAL

We went to visit the graveyard,
where you shared tales of your ghosts
and brushes with mortality,
asking me to join you in looking at a grave site.
Then, as we wander the grass,
you told me about your plans
for your gravestone inscription,
and when we arrived
you never told me it had my name too.
You tried to bury me with you,
but forgot coffins only hold one person,
so I tossed my flowers on the ground
and walked away.

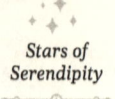
Stars of Serendipity

WEIGHING EMOTIONS

Which is heavier
seven pounds of grief
or seven pounds of remorse?

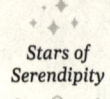

RESILIENT RELAPSE

Letting go
doesn't mean
it did not affect you,
it means that
you will not let it affect you again.

*Amelia E.
Eric-Markovic*

NEW TIMES, NEW ASHES

Looking at the seconds
feels good
when I am counting down the memories
till they lower your casket
and I can finally live
pt.III

Stars of Serendipity

GRAVE FAREWELL

I have more living people that are dead to me then dead people living through me.

The Kind

In a world often bustling with self-interest, encountering genuinely kind individuals who embody empathy remind us that even slight gestures create ripples of love and understanding. They serve as an invitation to humanity's compassionate nature, urging reflection on encounters with kindness and the potential for change. Through remarkable individuals, we become a testament to the enduring power of love, compassion, and the innate goodness that nests within the heart.

CHERRY TREE

I miss my Baba's cherry tree.
We walk into the backyard
and pluck them as we talk.
We don't understand each other very well,
her first language is flowers
and mine is melodies.
But, we both interpret dance:
the sway in her flowers
from the ballads of the breeze,
rocking roses, capering carnations,
and hopping hydrangeas.
The foliage frolicking in the ballroom of her garden
as the wind and birds provide a hurricane
of harmony in an otherwise peaceful place.

Amelia E.
Eric-Markovic

EMBRACE

A small town can be smothering
but the big city can be suffocating
and I would rather support
a tight hug
than a choke hold.

Stars of Serendipity

KEEPSAKE

Souvenirs help us remember
that wherever we go
we can always bring a piece of it home.
Cities on sweaters are a reminder
that we can carry communities with us
and keychains turn into traveled treasures.
Mementos let us move with moments
instead of moving on from memories.

Amelia E.
Eric-Markovic

"SELF-CARE"

Please stop taking off your band-aids
to cover the wounds of others.
Wrap yourself up tight, take your meds
and douse in ointments.
No one will help you if you do not help yourself,
because playing doctor is easier than admitting pain.

Stars of Serendipity

NURTURING SERENITY

Tranquillity arises
when nurturing your soul
becomes instinct,
and serenity takes control.
Your spirit becomes the secretary
that takes in the calls of the universe
and you are left with cruise control divinity.

*Amelia E.
Eric-Markovic*

TRIAL BY TOWER

We walked up all the stairs
of your ivory-covered skyscraper.
Hand-in-hand, as we approached the ledge.
And then you watched me.
I looked down at the ground beneath my feet
and welcomed you to sit down.
As I pointed out our houses in the distance,
you showed me the place we first met.
Although the breeze was refreshing,
not being asked to jump was rejuvenating.

Stars of Serendipity

COMPASSION COSTUME

You can walk in my shoes
as far as you want.
But take my jacket,
my socks and my jeans,
and take my shirt and glasses.
Wear me for a day not a mile,
be seen as I have,
be talked to like I am,
be heard from my voice.
If you do not like it
you are the problem.
If it is familiar
you are a recipient.
If it is eye-opening
you are the change.

Stars of Serendipity

SEEING XX

The only thing I have ever heard from a man
who took the time to ask his female coworkers
if they had to 'just deal with it'
was an apology.
Men taking the time to realize that women
deal with a lot more than we need to
and that we 'just deal with it'
was a signal that maybe men
never have to put up with things
if they don't want to hang them.

*Amelia E.
Eric-Markovic*

RETURNING TIME

Moments of gratitude are the receipts we make throughout our life. Moments of greed or when we try to return what life gave us for something better.

Stars of Serendipity

GIVING THIEVES

I have never known thieves to be givers.
When people say they have been robbed I have
never asked them what they were gifted
till I met you.
You broke into my house and tore through
the caution tape to hang flowers from the rafters.
You looted my pictures and put up new memories,
shoplifted my megaphones
after filling my halls with music,
and ran off with my couches
when you furnished your arms.
I grew apprehensive as you held my breath captive
but you traded it in for laughter.
Somehow you got into my closet
and smuggled my nightgowns for your T-shirts, and
my perfectly fitted hoodies were swapped by your
helicopter sleeves.
Then you found my attic,
purged it of its relics and souvenirs,
and bestowed its space.
Took the squeak out of the floorboards
that reminded me that my house wasn't perfect.

Amelia E.
Eric-Markovic

You broke into my house
and my alarms did not sound
for you took my house and provided me a home.
I have never known thieves to be givers,
because you were the repairer of my things.

Stars of
Serendipity

WORKING LIFE OUT

Finding out who you are
and why you are here now
is how you are going to be able to
work for love
and love to work.

*Amelia E.
Eric-Markovic*

WHISPERS OF PERCEPTION

We talked in a desolate restaurant
on a sun-drenched afternoon.
You couldn't believe my outlook on life,
complimenting how far beyond my years I was.
I didn't know if you were thanking the anxiety
for pushing me to such potential
or for giving me unrealistic ideas.
Maybe it was a shout-out to the times I have faced
that women in my field do not get as far.
It was a possible nod to my abilities
to be both the youngest in a room
and not juvenile.
But I like to think it was because
you watched my growth
as a student, a professional, a human
and realized that my listening
was always bigger than my actions.

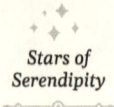
Stars of Serendipity

MIRROR REPRESENTATION

I ask to go to the bathroom and stare at the mirror.
When you want to see people like you
doing the things you are doing,
it must start with you.

*Amelia E.
Eric-Markovic*

BOTTLED ASPIRATIONS

I am ambitious
because there is no genie
following me around granting wishes,
until I look at my shadow.

*Amelia E.
Eric-Markovic*

WORKING MEMORY

Working on remembering a working man.
Remembering you in your uniform
but unable to picture you without it.
Recalling thirty-minute conversations
during your breaks,
I always thought they were too short,
but thirty minutes
seems like too much to ask for now.

Stars of Serendipity

SUBLIMINAL HELP

A hug with a tighter squeeze in the middle
Translation:
Thank you for this hug.
I needed it... Because I need you to know...
I love you,
and I am here for you.
Please, text me later
and tell me what's wrong.

*Amelia E.
Eric-Markovic*

CONNECTION LOADING

I promise
that the reason you stay today
will be the way people know you tomorrow.
You do not get what you deserve,
You attract what you accept.

Stars of Serendipity

SEASONS FEELINGS CHANGE

Going to bed
hoping to feel the same tomorrow
is like asking the weather
to be the same between seasons.
Asking for no change will deny you of
warmer days, blooming plants,
snowflakes, and leaf piles.

*Amelia E.
Eric-Markovic*

WAKING POSSESSION

Silk supports embrace the pillowed face
as warm blankets cradle the corpse.
Eyes fall slowly to the cargo of fatigue
providing the brain room to roam.
The mind is floating through dreams
and cascading into sleep.
Waking feels like a possession of the body
rising with the sun.

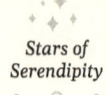
Stars of Serendipity

MEMORIES WALTZ

Comfort dancing is my favourite style.
I appreciate its wide usage and music options.
From dancing on couches,
to the embrace of a slow song,
it's forgiveness in toe-stepping,
and the ability to create memories
instead of rehearsed choreography.

Stars of Serendipity

THAT IS ALL

"Guess what?"
"What?"
"I love you."
"Is that all?"
"That is everything."

*Amelia E.
Eric-Markovic*

POWER OF LOVE

Illuminating my eyes,
your smile shone through the curtain of my bangs
and as we went through life,
you glowed through your skin
and I echoed in my laugh.
We powered each other through the darkest of days
till the morning you got that call,
your face dropped,
and then the power outage starts.
Our blackout lasted for weeks
both of us were powerless to each other.
Finally, months later, you lit a candle
and realized I was there for you all the time.
The dark can hide the light switch
yet its presence remains,
patiently awaiting to guide you back to illumination.

Amelia E.
Eric-Markovic

ROOTS OF MANHOOD

As much as a wonderful woman
raises a good man,
look at his father,
his brothers,
and his cousins.
Then you will know the man
he will become.

Stars of Serendipity

PRESENTLY PAST IT

You look at me and see the people you have hurt.
I look at you and see the people that have hurt me.
All the same trauma.
None of the continuation.

*Amelia E.
Eric-Markovic*

ORIGAMI CONVERSATIONS

Listening is hard
when the ear is one fold away from being a swan.
You look at me
like my words caused the creases
and yet I only know how to make stars.
So I repeat my words
as you undo the folds
and we talk
with open ears.

Stars of Serendipity

THORNLESS BLOOMS

Seeing you strip away
all your thorns
as we grow together
helped me watch your
petals bloom
instead of being
scared to get close to you.

Stars of Serendipity

DEVOTED LUMINARY

A ball of light,
I find myself often comparing
my warmth to the stars.
How my alignment with you creates art in the sky,
I cannot die when I am so far away from Earth
that it would take years to see the light fade,
and that is how I know the grandkids will speak
of our devotion.

You will not always see my starry love,
cause when everything is bright it is hard to see
what is there for you in the dark.
But I want my star to be your sun,
burning brightly to melt away
your snowdrifts of sorrow
and put colour back into your scenery.
And even if my glow diminishes,
I am content in knowing I will be a star
among your night sky,
to comfort you in dark times.

Amelia E.
Eric-Markovic

TIMELY ACKNOWLEDGEMENTS

Thinking about five or ten years from now,
I ask myself if you would still be around
if I depleted into the depths of depression
or rose to the ravishings of riches.

I work to earn all that is not here
cause if it can come in five years
then why can't I try it now,
when the only thing time is doing for me
is fleeting.

When entering a new chapter in our lives,
it should be habitual to thank those around us,
and strive for more within us.

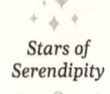

Stars of Serendipity

SIDUS SALUTATIONS

A universe of creation
galaxies of innovation
and yet humans all still meet the same way.
A greeting followed by a smile,
a handshake,
or a fist bump
and then questions;
"How are you doing?",
"Isn't the weather lovely?",
"What do you do?".
But I yearn to meet the same as stars,
distant at first,
glowing and bright with confidence
in the right place, at the right time.
A connection forms a constellation,
a zodiac created from our time together.
The most beautiful relationship
is woven in the sky.
People will gaze up at our nexus
and wonder how to get next to us.
We will inspire with the ability to
burn on the coldest of days

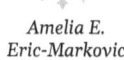

*Amelia E.
Eric-Markovic*

and glimmer while the sun is still setting
because constellations like this
don't form every millennium.
And when you leave the sky,
when your light fades from my side,
our affinity will shine forever.

Stars of Serendipity

ANGEL'S EXIT

"Talk to you later, Love You Lots"
The last words of the card you sent me
for my 18th birthday.
I saved the card until you had passed.
XXXOOO

The Contemplator

In the tapestry of our lives, there exist those who ignite curiosity and beckon us to embark on profound introspective journeys. These inspiring individuals challenge our perspectives, fostering self-reflection and contemplation. Through their connections, we unravel life's mysteries, cultivate boundless curiosity, and gain profound insights. This intellectual bid to embrace introspection enriches our understanding of human existence, empowering us to navigate the complexities of our world with newfound wisdom.

Stars of Serendipity

POINTING BACK

Suing everyone is easy
until the jury delivers the conviction
in the form of a mirror.

*Amelia E.
Eric-Markovic*

PARALLEL POTENTIALS

In another life,
I may be done with school.
In the next dimension,
there could be a nice car in my driveway.
In another universe,
you could find me in my corner office.
Nothing compares to possibly being
the worst version of yourself.

Stars of Serendipity

PROUD PARTY

Validation is the friend that comes along
when overlooking has done its damage
but left a person in tears.
Pride arrives when failure has left the room
and disappointment didn't crash the party.
Praise can creep in, but only with an invitation
and maybe, someday,
I will see self-assured and bragging
if I make it through this year unscathed.

Amelia E. Eric-Markovic

FEEL, FEELING, FELT

Are you trying to feel something,
are you trying to feel nothing,
or are you trying to feel the way you used to feel?

HARD PILL

Can we start trying to swallow awareness
in the form of healing
before overdosing on escapism
in the form of hiding.

*Amelia E.
Eric-Markovic*

GRIEVING NOTHING

Longing
is the grieving process
for something
you cannot have.

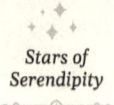
Stars of Serendipity

SIDING WITH SHAPES

My edges did not fit
through the opening meant for circles,
and yet too few to be a hexagon.
Angles set me apart from rectangles
although our sides matched.
So, I went to the triangles to compare.
With certain angles matching
we found solace for a while,
but it's hard to take the same side
when you have more.

*Amelia E.
Eric-Markovic*

PERSONAL PURGE

Growing up is easier than growing.
Changing sizes and styles
while getting rid of old clothes
feels like a purge of your old self.
Changing personalities and mannerisms
while watching old friends leave
feels like a purge of yourself.

*Amelia E.
Eric-Markovic*

GIFTS OF EXISTENCE

Life and Living
are two different things.
Life is a gift
presented to us
by God.
Living is a gift
presented to us
by ourselves.

Stars of Serendipity

IDLE AVENUE

Stood in the middle of the street
watching people pass
I realized other people's lives are easier to look at
then your own.
But maybe that's why it is also relaxing.
To sit back and watch God's work:
knowing that reflection can be in others
before you make it in yourself.

*Amelia E.
Eric-Markovic*

CALLING 463

We call for help with phones,
light signals in the sky,
radios, and cries.
I call for you through the tip of my fingers
pressed softly on my temple,
to my chest,
then passing to my shoulders.
I like to pray facing walls
because that is what talking to you feels like.
Wondering if you are there
or if I am loud enough.

Stars of Serendipity

STANDING UP

Beliefs are the barefoot
of which we stand up
for what has been destroyed by everyone else.
pt.I

*Amelia E.
Eric-Markovic*

MUSICAL FEELINGS

When did mean versus lose meaning?
Seeing yourself in the mirror of the melody,
relapsing in the reverb.
We would call musicians 'doctors'
for their remedies,
their potion from a point of view,
for a drug of deep thought.
So, now I dig through the prescriptions of my past
for the ache of appeal,
for lyrics with lessons,
but it's easy to flat-line when you lost emotions
before the music did.

Stars of Serendipity

LESSONS OF RECIPROCITY

Learning from students
should be a requirement for teachers.
How else are you going to see
the bigger lessons you are instructing?

*Amelia E.
Eric-Markovic*

GLORIOUS SOLITUDE

Finding silence is hard
when it's easier to escape a crowd than your mind.

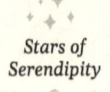

Stars of Serendipity

OPEN A BOOK

Running away
to another place and comfort people
is not a bad thing
if you never left.
Cushioned between the cream pages,
there is something comforting about
experiencing another life
at any moment
when your existence
feels like too much.

Stars of Serendipity

PHONE BOOK

The hardest part
of being your own biggest support
is the absence of voicemail,
when no one's there to call.

*Amelia E.
Eric-Markovic*

GROWING PAINS

Placed on the tip of my pinkie,
the world seems small and delicate yet sturdy.
Time weighed on my perceptions
and worries made you grow.
Suddenly my palms grasped the equator
like a handle
steadying its force against my collarbones,
rolling over my shoulder,
my back became a seat and I the hunchback.
The world is not a forgiving place
but neither is my spine.
Placed gently back in orbit,
I apologize,
for I could not grow with you.

*Amelia E.
Eric-Markovic*

STAND ALONE

Morals are the spine
of which we are held up
for what has been abandoned by everyone else.
pt.II

Stars of Serendipity

CAVING CHIPPED

When our hands rise,
chins lowered to our chests,
the weights crumble,
released from our burdened shoulders.
Surrender feels good at first
until your ego and morals cave in and
crush your pride as they plunder
through your knees.
Spirits fleet
as the soul abandons the chest
yet emptiness crawls in.
Sacrifice aids in releasing
the weight of the problem;
hollow humans cannot stand for themselves.

*Amelia E.
Eric-Markovic*

SYNONYMS FOR STUDENT

Expensive broke people are a rare breed.
Swallowing dreams at every meal
and wearing the future on their skin.
Working for the car they don't have
and returning to a home that is not theirs.

Stars of Serendipity

INTRINSIC TREASURES

Gold holds a greater value in my eyes
than its mere price,
for heirlooms possess a weight in generations
that transcends any worth measured in carats.

*Amelia E.
Eric-Markovic*

A STEP ABOVE

It's hard to look
at others' success
when the footstool
faces down.

Stars of Serendipity

GASLIGHTING ORANGE

"Red."
I answer every time someone asked for
my favourite colour.
But in all truth, I have been depriving orange.
Orange rising in the morning with the new horizon
and escaping with the sun
for whatever fun they have past my view.
The warmest light comes from caramel halos
crowning everyday saints
and burning paper in fires.
Sweetness sugars the tongue
after an encounter with Orange,
who graces it with friends
clementine, tangerine, and apricot.
Orange grows in carrots through the dirt,
loving in vermilion on the lips of strangers
and aging in rust on beloved items.

Orange is living
thriving,
and dying
devoid of appreciation.

*Amelia E.
Eric-Markovic*

PAPER ECHOES

When I lose myself,
I go through the cards I have been given.
Searching for the person they were talking to.
These memories of birthdays and holidays
only remind me of how much
I want to go
forwards
or
backwards.

Stars of Serendipity

PASSING ANXIETIES

Before I pass, tell them how much I worried.
Extrapolate my fears from my soul,
relay all the times when I proved
again and again
that I would do everything possible
to make things right,
Because you can't fear failure this much
if you aren't trying to succeed.
Let them know I succeeded.
Tell them about my family and career,
my passions and my persistence.
Convince them of my growth
after telling them how short I am.
Before I go,
help me persuade myself that the constant anxiety
helped me live life a little more.

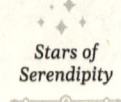

Stars of Serendipity

GLASS CROWN

Placed on my head
delicate and precisely,
held high and steady.
I am proud to serve my people
who have fallen so many times to
fragile favouritism.
Those in second place after one mistake
and grieving love following a slip-up.
Perfection is in the eye of the beholder,
but the only clarity I have been given on that
sits on my crown.

*Amelia E.
Eric-Markovic*

PLASTER CONTRACTS

Signing my casts
is the contract of helping me heal.
Maybe that's why,
with age,
the plaster bears fewer names.

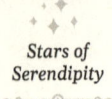
Stars of Serendipity

REMOVING MYSELF

Constant change
only works if they are all positive.
And relocating is easy
when you are not the one with baggage.

*Amelia E.
Eric-Markovic*

GOING FORWARD

"I have to get going."
"No, stay here with me."
Until you want to keep my future
you cannot hold my present.

Stars of Serendipity

SERENDIPITY

The encounters of gold we are gifted
by chance, by the universe, by God.
These are the flowers left on our doorstep,
or the random sticky notes
we are presented:
to remind us
that we are worth
the life we are living;
in all of its essence.

Stars of Serendipity

ABOUT THE AUTHOR

Amelia E. Eric-Markovic, a debut poet from Ontario, Canada, presents "Stars of Serendipity," a heartfelt collection of poetry that delves into the connections she has forged with others and herself. Currently pursuing an Advanced Diploma in Computer Programming and Analysis at Durham College, Amelia infuses her writing with personal observations and experiences, revealing the transformative power of poetic expression. When not immersed in the world of poetry or coding, she finds solace in music, podcasts, and the calming embrace of water. Follow Amelia on TikTok for updates on her writing journey and discover the wonders of life through the captivating power of 'Stars of Serendipity,' her riveting debut collection.

You can connect with Amelia at:
Website: https://ameliaeric.github.io
Tiktok: @aeem_tiktok

www.ingramcontent.com/pod-product-compliance
Lightning Source LLC
Chambersburg PA
CBHW031122080526
44587CB00011B/1077